BEYOND BOOKKEEPING

BEYOND BOOKKEEPING

How to

PARTNER WITH YOUR CLIENTS,
ADD TREMENDOUS VALUE,

and

BUILD A PROFITABLE BUSINESS
THAT MATTERS

Lisa Campbell

Niche Pressworks

BEYOND BOOKKEEPING

ISBN-13: 978-1-952654-27-5 Paperback
978-1-952654-26-8 eBook

Published by Niche Pressworks: http://NichePressworks.com

Dedication

This book is dedicated to the incredible bookkeepers, accountants, and EAs I've had the pleasure of working with as part of the Accelerate 2 Advisor community. You are paving the way for those coming after you. I'm truly inspired by your enthusiasm, hard work, and dedication to making a change for yourselves, your families, and your clients.

As you travel this leg of your journey, I'm honoured to be with you, and I'll share my daily mantra in the hope it may also serve you:

I expand in abundance, love, and success every day while inspiring others to do the same.

Contents

Testimonials

This book is for accountants who believe working too hard for too little is just part of the job. This book not only gives them the hope and vision for a completely different (and way more desirable) situation, it also provides very hands-on, easy-to-implement steps. Steps which, once implemented, immediately account for more time, more joy, more fulfilment, more money, or all of those.

—Femke Hogema, author of *The Profit Advisor* and Head of Profit First Professionals Netherlands

I met Lisa in 2019 when I started my journey as a Profit First Professional. Since then, I have participated in development programs, subscribed to Lisa's programs, and worked with her in different capacities. What has remained consistent through all of my dealings with Lisa is the knowledge, professionalism, and integrity she maintains in everything she does. Lisa's generosity and genuine desire to see business owners in our industry thrive is refreshing. Her ability to cut through all the noise and lay out a clear path for bookkeepers and accountants to transition to advisory guarantees success. Not a light promise, but she delivers every time.

—Emily Tarney

Founder, Competitive Edge Business Solutions Inc.

I first met Lisa at a conference in September 2019. I was aware of Lisa's success within her own business using the strategies she taught in A2A mastermind. I wanted to change my accounting practice from being totally compliant into a systemized business that would not need me 24/7, so I could concentrate on offering and implementing advisory services to clients who wanted to be profitable and have greater financial security. Lisa and her team gave me the knowledge and assistance to do so. They were there every step of the way, providing the guidance and support to implement these changes. I have taken many courses for business and personal development, but none provided ALL the tools you need to put the pieces of the puzzle together. It's a work in progress, but with Lisa's encouragement and support, I now have the mindset and knowledge to make the necessary changes. I thoroughly encourage anyone who wants to have freedom and a financially successful business to work with Lisa Campbell and her team at A2A mastermind.

—Carla DiFranco
CPA, Jordi Accounting & Tax

I first saw Lisa on a free Facebook masterclass. To say she provided extreme value would be an understatement. I eventually joined her mastermind program. When I first started my business, I had hired a business coach. What Lisa gives in her group is beyond anything I ever got in one-on-one sessions with that coach. She brings kindness, generosity, and giving. I have never felt so much support from somebody.

—Michele Ball
CMA, CFM, Your CFO Solutions

I was first introduced to Lisa Campbell when I did her Accelerator Method Masterclass. I didn't know who she was or what she was delivering and wasn't committed to completing nine days of training. After the first session, though, I knew this was something different and unlike anything I had encountered before. Her energy, enthusiasm, and knowledge were over-the-top amazing! I returned EVERY day, and by the end, I knew the program was exactly what I needed to take my bookkeeping business to the next level…and beyond. Prior to meeting Lisa, I knew I wanted systems, and I knew I wanted automation. What I didn't know was what to use, where to find it, or how to implement it while running my business. Lisa has it figured out. Now, the implementation is getting done one step at a time. It is a lot of work, but the payoff is a smooth, stress-free operation with clear processes for me and my team and, of course, exceptional and consistent service for our clients. Thank you, Lisa!

—Stephanie Kelcey
Owner, Capture Bookkeeping Inc.

Lisa's program is a deliberate roadmap that addresses the challenges facing our industry. At just five months into the program, my firm is almost completely systemized, meaning my team can independently process client work without my assistance!!! This has made it possible to survive unanticipated staff changes without returning to 15-hour workdays!! I am beyond grateful for the community Lisa has created and the vision of future potential she has instilled in me.

—Rae Gagnon
Owner, Blue Jean Business Solutions

Since we started working with Lisa, our expenses are down more than 60 percent, and our net profit has increased by $40,000 per month. Most importantly, I finally have a reliable, consistent system for growing that profit every single month. I don't see us ever managing our finances any other way.

—Taylor Allen
Deep Game Inc.

I found Lisa Campbell, and she has been a huge asset to my business. Because I had been working with her for almost a full year prior to COVID-19 shutdowns, I was able to successfully navigate closures and government programs while continuing to move forward toward goals I set for my company and my family. Lisa continues to provide great counsel that is always current and implementable now! I definitely recommend this type of business coaching for anyone who needs help finding direction in their books and finances. I am so grateful to have this type of mentorship and coaching behind me in such times as we are in now.

—Tara Pickford
Ambition Performing Arts Academy Inc.

Lisa has been an invaluable part of our journey from technicians to advisors. Thanks to Lisa's resources, advice, and support throughout the process, we were able to automate our processes, increase productivity, and free up time. These changes allow us to focus on adding more value to our clients.

—Katryna Coltess
Founder, Plus Associates Bookkeeping

As a professional bookkeeper, I was always struggling to keep up with client demands while trying to help them make the best decisions for their businesses. Now, after working with Lisa and her Accelerate 2 Advisor program, my firm is systemized to the point that I can hand off the compliance work and focus on bringing my clients the high-level advisory support they deserve. Lisa's coaching has been instrumental in not only developing the processes in my business but in changing my whole mindset around my ability to achieve great things for my clients as well as me!

—Michelle Krieger
CPB, PFP, Dragonfly Ventures Ltd.

Because of Lisa's mentoring, we have implemented her recommended project management software, which has enabled us to streamline our processes, meet industry standards, and raise our rates. These changes resulted in our firm doubling our annual revenue in 2020! With Lisa, I feel like I have a true friend and mentor in the industry, helping me to level up my firm and create the life I've always desired but felt unattainable. Lisa has helped me create a future vision I know I can obtain. I am grateful for her ability to see my potential and her ability to help ME see my potential. My firm will never be the same!

—Kisha Johnson
Owner, Your Numbers Nerd LLC

Introduction

"Oh shit! Did I remember to do that?"

It's the middle of the night on July 31, 2014.

I've been awakened from a deep sleep with the sudden realization that the return for one of my long-standing clients was due to the Canada Revenue Agency by midnight.

I was certain I had cross-checked all the important points and had submitted the return. Or had I? Had I been so wrapped up in the rescue project I was doing for my new, nonprofit client that I'd forgotten?

I crawl out of bed and fire up my laptop.

Damn, I didn't submit it.

I hadn't even done the pre-work to be able to file it. There goes another day of vacation.

Did I mention that I was on vacation with my family at the lake? This was supposed to be my downtime, when I could finally enjoy some quality time with my kids, soaking up nature and the beach at our cottage.

By morning, I'm still sitting in front of my laptop, struggling to get a strong enough internet connection to finish the work and file the damn return. Through the window, I can see my family head down to the beach while I'm staring at yet another spreadsheet. At that moment, as I watched them go without me, I swore to myself, *"I'll never miss another minute with my kids while we're on vacation."*

Of course, I'd made that promise to myself before—many times. But "urgent" work always seemed to pop up at the last minute.

I'd always think to myself, "People who have a 'job' get vacations—actual time off with pay. Since I have the 'freedom' of running my own business, I should be able to set my own schedule and workload."

But then I'd realize…if I don't do the work, deadlines will be missed, I won't get paid, and my clients will be pissed off. So I keep working. This return wasn't going to get done by itself.

Before leaving, my kids had pleaded, "Mom, come swimming with us!"

As usual, I replied, "I'll be right there. I just have to finish this first."

Then, as always, three hours later, I'd hit the beach when they were all tapped out. My (soon to be ex-) husband would look at me sideways and make some crack about my clients being more important than my family. He'd comment about the number of hours I put in compared to the bank balance. "Why are your client's needs so important? They don't even pay you that much."

"It's my job," was all I could say.

"Is this what being in business is supposed to look like?" I'd ask myself. Always on, always available, always in a state of overwhelm? Chasing money that was owed to me, justifying my invoices, dealing with pain-in-the-ass clients, and never being able to just turn it off?

Lightbulb moment: I had a job, not a business.

I had a high-stress job that only I could do. A job that didn't allow me time off, let alone paid time off. Something had to change. I needed a SYSTEM.

I knew systemizing was something successful businesses did. But what was there to systemize?

"I'm a bookkeeper," I thought. "I just do all the work myself, and then I get paid. (Well, most of the time, and it's usually not enough.)

"But what if there was some way to systemize what I do? To keep my deadlines straight, get myself out of panic mode, and possibly hand off some of the work to someone else?"

The problem was, I didn't have the time or the wherewithal to come up with my own system. I discovered I could simply buy a system that would do exactly what I needed, but I didn't have the money. My future ex would never approve of this spend, and thanks to his can't-keep-a-job-so-let's-just-borrow-more approach to finances, we were already drowning in debt.

My gut told me it was time to take action, and I was the only one who was going to turn this around. Apart from the stress of my work and finances, I also knew I needed to leave him. There was no way I could continue the way things were going.

I secretly ordered the systemization program I needed. I remember when it arrived—two boxes full of templates, binders, and manuals! I pulled everything out of the boxes, removed the labels, and shoved everything into nameless white binders. I packed down the boxes and hid them in the back of my truck.

Now it was up to me to get the ROI. I had to do the work to set up these systems and create something amazing out of nothing. This was going to be my ticket to freedom, both financially and mentally.

I worked tirelessly—on my client work and on putting these systems in place. I gave up even more time with my kids, along with meals, sleep, and any personal downtime. Deep down, I knew I was working on something that would create independence for me (and my kids).

I systemized all my compliance work and brought each of my clients into the process I was developing. This ensured the work I did going forward would be consistent and manageable, no matter what type of business they owned or what I had done with them in the past.

All my work began to pay off. Soon, I was able to raise my rates, so I hired my first team member. That allowed me to delegate some of the work, confident that the systems I had put in place would ensure that the work was done correctly and on time.

I stopped working evenings and weekends—and at last, I had the time with my kids I had longed for. In fact, the system became so effective I ended up having extra time on my hands.

Eventually, I had a process in place for everything my company did. I designed an entirely new client intake system—changing how I onboarded new clients, how we handled the work, etc. No more pain-in-the-ass clients, and no more wasted time on phone calls and emails. I now worked only with clients I wanted to work with, ones who valued what my company brought to the table and who automatically paid me upfront and on time.

But as great as all this was for both my business and my sanity, I realized my company was still exchanging time for money. We were still seen by clients as simply an expense, taking care of compliance task by task.

With all my years of experience, I knew I had so much more I could offer my clients. I wanted them to see me as a partner, someone who was a necessary part of their team, who actually made a difference to their business.

So, I began studying profitability and cash flow. I acquired the skills necessary to provide a solution for the number one problem business owners face: *never having enough money.*

I learned how to position this new skill as a vital part of the relationship I had with my clients. I learned how to get paid for it—and paid very well. And I learned how to make a *difference.*

As a result of making all these changes, life is very different these days.

I work from home, so I'm there for my kids. (And yes, I left my husband. I now had the financial means and the time to support my children.)

My team has grown. They handle the compliance work and all the other behind-the-scenes responsibilities, so I no longer have to coordinate every detail. Better yet, I never go into a discovery call with the intention of selling; rather, my intent is to serve. I work only with those who see the value in everything we provide. I charge my clients based on that value, not on the time a specific project may take. And, best of all, I never have to chase receivables.

Now that I'm an *advisor* to my clients, I am debt-free. (I had lost everything and started over at age 46.) I pay my taxes on time, every time, and I take a regular salary plus a profit distribution from my company.

Evenings and weekends are mine to do with what I choose. And when I go on vacation, I leave work at home.

Most importantly, I've shown my children that you can overcome any obstacle with desire, a plan, action, and confidence in what you can achieve.

Back when I was that anxious and overworked bookkeeper who had to spend her family vacations tied to her laptop, I felt there was no way out of the life I was living. But then I found a doorway to a new way of working and living that made my life my own.

If you have the same desire for more time, more money, and more freedom in your work and your life, this book will lead you through that same door and guide you on the path to achieving what you want.

My hope is that the ideas in this book will be useful at any stage of your bookkeeping career. For those of you who are new to bookkeeping, a lot of this may not resonate with you yet, but keep these principles in mind as you work, and keep the book handy for when you're a couple of years into growing your business. You'll need it then!

For experienced bookkeepers, especially if your roster is full and you're really NOT loving your work, then you're ready—this book is for you!

Chapter 1

REMAIN A BOOKKEEPER OR LEVEL UP TO FREEDOM

You have the huge opportunity to gain a lot more time, freedom, and money by relying on your bookkeeping background…and it's not that hard to do!

If you had told me years ago that I would NOT be the one doing the day-to-day work at my firm, I would have dismissed it. If you'd told me I'd be charging premium fees and only working with ideal clients who valued my relationship and the work I do, I would have thought you were off your rocker. After all, I was just a bookkeeper. I didn't have a degree in finance.

How could I have gone from providing a commodity that was an expense most business owners didn't want to pay for to a specialist who became an integral part of their decision-making process? The answer: I specialized in an aspect of their business that really needed attention—profitability and cash flow!

Think of it this way. I bet that if you were to call your doctor's office today, you could probably get an appointment within the week. But, if you needed to see a specialist, you might have to wait for months. Why is that?

Specialists obtain advanced training in very specific areas. Let's look at cardiac surgeons. After completing a surgical residency, they continue their training with a focus on thoroughly researching and learning everything to do with the heart. They know heart anatomy, how it works, what can go wrong with it, and how to fix it better than anyone else.

Sure, they could also prescribe something for heartburn or migraines. They could even do your annual physical, but that's not why people wait months to see them.

If you or a loved one was suffering from a terminal heart condition, would you want your general practitioner to operate, or would you fly across the country, at any cost, for the cardiac surgeon?

The same principle applies to you. Are you the same bookkeeper you were when you first started out? What if you took the experience you already have, expanded upon it, and specialized in an industry, process, or solution?

That's how you become a specialist. Bookkeepers are generalists. But bookkeepers who use their experience to focus on a specific area become specialists. Gone are the days when forward-thinking entrepreneurs simply do their books for compliance and filing their taxes! We, who are closest to their numbers, need to use our years of experience to become key players in their day-to-day decision-making process and problem resolution.

Advise clients using the story their numbers tell.

What if, rather than taking on every client and spending your day coding and reporting, you could actually make a difference in the way a business runs?

LEVELLING UP

There's a shift in our industry, and it's happening right now. Business owners need more, and cutting-edge bookkeepers are providing it to them.

Let's look at a typical year in the accounting cycle. The accountant is working on what happened last year. The bookkeeper is working on what happened last month. The business owner is looking at what's happening today. But what's happening tomorrow, in the next six months, or even in the coming year?

This is simply a matter of examining, planning, and strategizing about cash flow to help the client move their business forward. But in my experience, most bookkeepers are not inserting themselves into the situation to become part of the solution.

For me, this was one of the biggest challenges my clients faced—a constant struggle with profitability, cash flow, and stopping the cycle of never-ending debt. I was bound and determined to find a way to help them.

In 2017, I began looking at the most common struggle my own clients had: cash flow. There was never enough cash, and they were always robbing Peter to pay Paul. We see it all the time! Constant borrowing, struggling to meet payroll, accounts payable out of control, and more often than not, the business owner rarely getting paid regularly, never mind being paid what they should.

Then, I came across an incredible book by Mike Michalowicz, *Profit First*. According to Michalowicz, 83 percent of small businesses live cheque-to-cheque, struggling to make ends meet. OMG! These were my clients!

It took me six months to become certified as a Profit First Professional.[1] I developed the skills to apply Profit First principles to businesses and to coach my clients through strategies and obstacles.

Little by little, I concentrated my efforts on attracting only those clients who wanted help with cash flow. Simultaneously, I disengaged from small clients who only wanted compliance work done.

The result? I transformed my bookkeeping business into a profit strategy firm. My team does the bookkeeping, and I am the advisor.

Even though profit strategy became MY specialty, yours

---

1 Profit First Professionals is a global organization with highly skilled bookkeepers, accountants, and business coaches certified in the Profit First methodology who support entrepreneurs far beyond what is explained in the book. Go to profitfirstprofessionals.ca (Canada), profitfirstprofessionals.nl (Netherlands), profitfirstaustralia.com.au (Australia), www.profit-first.de (Germany), and profitfirstprofessionals.com (USA and the rest of the globe).

might be something entirely different from cash flow or profitability. Regardless of what you choose to advise in, the process is the same.

> *Within six months of offering advisory services, my company has added over $100K in new revenue. Most importantly, I love being of service to my clients.*
> —SUSANNE MARIGA, MARIGA CPA

I belong to many groups of bookkeepers who have levelled up to advise their clients at premium rates.

It is the norm to see profits in their firms increase 200, 400, or even 600 percent compared to when they were just offering bookkeeping services. They've gone from hourly rates to annual contracts equating to $1000–$5000+ per month.

> *I've increased my company's net income by more than 400 percent! And my favourite part is that I've more than doubled my personal monthly take-home pay.*
> —TRACY JEPSON, TLJ CONSULTING

Why do specialists see this boost in profits? Because they provide results that demand those fees.

> *My company has experienced an increase in revenue and a massive jump in profitability—up 244 percent in one year!*
> —DAMON YUDICHAK, IDEAL MONEY LIFE

On the other side of the coin, their clients also see the same increases in their bottom lines. They don't hesitate to pay these significantly higher fees because they see the results. How rewarding is that?

No one has your particular insight to help a business owner move forward. You can rely on this understanding to make decisions based on what's happening now and what's about to happen. You, as the bookkeeper, are closest to the numbers. You understand what they mean and can relay that to your clients.

When you specialize, life is transformed for you and your clients. So let's get real about it here. This is what actually happens:

WHY YOU SHOULD BUILD YOUR PRACTICE TO OFFER ADVISORY SERVICES

The many benefits of becoming an advisor include:

- Create your own schedule, with greater flexibility over how you spend your work and personal time.
- Delegate the hamster wheel of compliance work to your team and focus on advising your clients.
- Become a vital part of your clients' teams because they value your input.
- Stop exchanging time for money and start exchanging VALUE for money (and a lot more of it!).
- Create positive change and impact for your clients.
- Choose the clients you work with—no more pain-in-the-ass clients (PITAs)!
- Earn income consistency at a significantly higher level.

3 WAYS TO GET WHERE YOU WANT TO BE

We all know that a business's books are crucial to understanding what's going on. They absolutely must be done accurately to provide critical information for running a successful company. But that doesn't mean YOU have to be the one doing them.

When you take the leap to specialize, you have a choice to make. You can:

1. Keep doing the compliance work that's already consuming all of your time and add your specialty to your client services. In this scenario, you continue to charge by the hour, taking on more clients to make more money—effectively doubling your workload.
2. Partner with another team. The other team does the compliance component, and you'll have time to specialize. You'll make a bit more money but will open yourself up to liability, delays, poor quality, reduced margins, and overall increased misery.
3. Evolve your business and focus only on your specialty business. In this case, you design your current business to bring on a team to handle the compliance work so that you focus on providing much higher-value service to your clients. You can see how this solution serves you and your family, which is why I did it. I'll show you how to do it in this book.

HOW I DID IT

In my firm, I only work with a maximum of 12 clients at a time. Time on my calendar is high-value real estate, and

I organize it in a way that aligns with my personal goals.

For me, that means I've designed my business around my personal life instead of the other way around. My family comes first. I'm not chained to my desk. I provide actual results and get paid for the value received instead of the time it takes to process transactions (how rewarding is that?).

If you're sitting there thinking, "Lisa, I bill out at $25 per hour. There's no way I can change my business the way you suggest!" I call BS. I've done it. I've shown my mastermind members they can do it, and I'll show you how to do it too.

Yes, it takes work. Yes, you need to spend time ON your business instead of always IN it. But the effort is worth it, many times over.

This is a short book. It's intended to open your mind to new possibilities for your business by revealing what others and I have done to transform the way we operate. Obviously, I can't hold your hand and walk you through every little detail in such a short amount of writing space. Nor can I guarantee anyone who replicates our process will achieve the same results we have.

I do, however, know a proven path to get to where you want to go—a process that puts you leaps and bounds ahead of all those bookkeepers trying to figure it out on their own.

It's time to get out of your own way. Time to step up and move forward toward creating the life you want. The industry is changing—and you can either evolve or fall behind and remain a commodity. I'll show you what's possible and how it's done. Whether or not it happens is up to you.

Chapter 2
HOW TO GIVE YOURSELF A RAISE—RIGHT NOW!

Jennifer sat at her desk, staring at several piles of mundane work. Through her office window, she could see her husband and son having a blast in the pool, enjoying the sunshine that seemed to be taunting her.

A self-admitted procrastinator, she knew time was running out. Deadlines were lurking, and she'd have to miss out on time with her young family yet again. She wondered how she could possibly get through the backlog of compliance work that had been haunting her for months. It had started when she landed a rescue project that she really enjoyed working on. The work was more complicated and better paying than her usual jobs, but it had taken time away from her regular clients. Even though compliance didn't pay very well and the clients were a pain to deal with, Jennifer knew the backlog of compliance work would remain a black cloud as long as it remained incomplete.

Almost in tears as she listened to what was going on in the backyard, Jennifer knew the only way to free up time for herself, get out of the overwhelm she was feeling, and most of all, make more money, would be to hire someone to help her.

It made sense, but she thought of all the disaster stories she'd heard from colleagues who had hired their own helpers:

- "They weren't as skilled as they claimed."
- "They ask too many questions."
- "You have to babysit them."
- "They don't do the work correctly."
- "Your clients only want you to do the work."

But this time, she just couldn't take it anymore. She had to take the plunge. She found Nicole, a pleasant woman with a lot of valuable experience. They immediately hit it off, and finally, Jennifer could breathe easier, knowing someone else was taking some of the load off—until three days later when Nicole resigned.

Now Jennifer was really depressed. She didn't know where to turn until a colleague suggested she reach out to me.

As she sat in her office on our first Zoom meeting, her entire body projected defeat.

"I've got so much work to do," she said. "I've got too many clients. Half the time, I'm chasing payments. I'm always working just to catch up, and I have no help for any of it."

"So why did Nicole quit?" I asked.

"She just didn't understand how I do things, and I didn't have time to stand over her and walk her through everything. Some of the clients I gave her to work on were only paying me $200 for an entire job, and she was taking hours to do the work. And she kept complaining that I didn't have any consistent processes to follow, and that's why she had to keep asking how to do things. Finally, she just gave up."

I told Jennifer I'd gone through problems and frustrations similar to what she was dealing with. "It sounds like there's a break in your ecosystem," I told her.

She gave me a puzzled look.

"The ecosystem of your business is how everything runs," I explained. "It starts by setting up internal systems that organize and structure what you do. These systems make it easy to hire someone in because it explains how you do things. The next benefit is that these systems help you get only the right clients. From the moment a potential client first contacts you, you follow a specific process to make sure you WANT to work with them.

"If you do, the process details how to onboard them and then determines how you and your team will systematically accomplish their work every month.

"Once your ecosystem is fully functioning, you'll start getting paid the fees you deserve for your work. The actual technical work can be done by someone else on your team, following a process that's the same for every client.

"Trust me, once you've systemized your operations this way, your clients will appreciate what you do even more, and you'll be able to spend your time focused on the valuable guidance you can offer your clients, not the mundane work that is overloading you."

I could see a hopeful expression start to appear on Jennifer's face until her predictable doubt crept in.

"That sounds like a dream," she said wistfully, "but I've already tried getting help. No one can take care of my clients the same way I do. Plus, I can't just pick and choose whatever clients I want. I pretty much have to take on anyone who can pay me just to stay afloat.

"And even if you could show me exactly what I'm doing wrong and how to fix it, where am I supposed to find the time? I'm already overloaded and backlogged. Maybe when things slow down a bit, we can talk again."

I didn't answer at first because I could see the look of defeat on her face.

Then I said, "Jennifer, let me ask you something. If you're struggling this much now, and you don't do anything to change your circumstances, where do you think you're going to be in a year from now?"

She thought about that for a few seconds, and then a look of determination appeared. "Okay," she said. "I'm in!"

MORE CLIENTS OR MORE VALUE?

As I tell the people in my classes, to get repositioned as an advisor and command the fees associated with that, the single most important thing we need to do is design our firm to **be of value** to the client!

Remember when you first started out? Hoping for prospects, trying to build your roster, and taking on anyone who would pay you for your services? You probably took a few fee cuts along the way as well, just to get clients signed. Little by little, I'll bet you also began offering some value-added services—review meetings, cash-flow forecasts, keeping an eye on their AP and AR, dropping what you're doing to tend to their "urgent" needs, etc. After all, to stand out as awesome and get those referrals, we want to give clients our all.

Of course, this is fine when dealing with only one or two clients. Satisfied clients give us referrals. But you're focused on attracting more clients with your strong reputation, which should result in more revenue.

As the business expands, you continue negotiating rates to attract new prospects. These clients receive the same stellar service offered to all your clients.

You're available, answering texts that come in at 10:00 p.m. and enduring idle chitchat that eats up chunks of the day. And let's not forget the requests for additional work that seem to just blend in with the regular work. You know, the "I need this application filled out for the bank" requests that will have you hunting down years' worth of information, assets, liabilities, FMV, and current balances.

Now, multiply that same scenario by 30 clients.

Finally, you start to realize that the line between personal time and work time has gotten hazy. Deadlines must be met, the work has to get done, and before you know it, long hours on evenings, weekends, and even holidays become the norm.

Still, we continue to believe that MORE clients will generate more money. But more clients mean we need more help, bigger facilities, more overhead, and more administrative costs. All of these cost more money, which means we need more clients…and so it goes.

But what if, rather than going for volume, we went for *value*? What if we could reduce the number of clients we look after, give them unbelievable value, and get them to pay us handsomely for it?

Okay, pay attention here because this is easier than you think. Grab your calculator and do this with me.

LET'S DO THE MATH

SCENARIO 1

You have 150 clients, with an average monthly bill of $250. That's $450K a year. Sounds great, right? But assuming a competent bookkeeper can handle about 30 clients per month, that's five full-time bookkeepers, including you. At $30 per hour, for example, that's $249,600 a year in wages for your four team members. Of that, you'll likely have at least another $50–60K in operating expenses. At that volume, you'll likely need some administrative support, so let's add another $30K for that. And you need to pay yourself, so we'll give you $75K. Pre-tax profit is $45,400.

Sounds pretty good, right? But now let's look at another option:

SCENARIO 2

You have only *10* clients, with an average monthly bill of $2,000. That's only $240K a year. But in this scenario, you only need *one* bookkeeper to do the compliance component for you, creating an annual cost of just $62,400. Gross profit:

$177,600. Add $50K for tech stack, administrative support, business development, etc., along with your $75K salary. Pre-tax profit: $52,600.

You've realized $7,200 more profit. And think how much better your life is!

> *Lisa helped me recognize that chasing revenue was a trap. I am already seeing huge benefits to my business and my clients' businesses.*
>
> —ANDREW ROYER, ROYER ACCOUNTING

IDENTIFYING YOUR VALUE

Dealing with PITA clients (at all hours of the day and for not enough money) is just part of the industry, right? Wrong. For some reason, we have a preconceived notion that the work we do is generic. There is a standard expectation—numbers in, numbers out. This has us believing we're doomed to stay stuck under a mountain of compliance work, charging by the hour or flat fee and trying to please everyone at the expense of our own sanity.

But think about it:

- You've built your business on your over-the-top service.
- You know exactly what needs to be done.
- You never miss a deadline.
- You know the story the numbers tell and can explain it to your clients.
- You know exactly how to rescue a disaster.
- Whatever the client needs, you're on it.

If you tell me what you do is "generic" or "standard," I'm not buying it.

One of the first obstacles many of the bookkeepers I work with have is identifying the value they can provide. I often hear them say, "I just do the books. Where's the value in that?"

Let me share the story of Sal from one of my mastermind groups. When he first started, he believed the same thing—until we completed an exercise that I'm about to share with you. Afterward, he had his first aha moment, exclaiming, "Now that's what I'm talking about! I have already tried value-based pricing, but I was using a crapshoot method! Now, I have a real tool. This is excellent!"

IDENTIFYING VALUE EXERCISE

Let's give this exercise a try. My aim is for you to have a little fun and gain a better idea of how your time is spent. So, grab a sheet of paper, and let's get started. Here's what you need to do:

1. Make a list of all the work you do right now that's strictly related to compliance (bank reconciliations, sales tax filings, payroll, month-end reporting, year-end preparation, etc.).
2. Then, at the bottom of the list, continue by adding everything you do in addition to compliance (review meetings, cash flow planning, specialized reports, deadline reminders, newsletters, etc.)
3. Below that, add to the list the things you consider when taking on and pricing work (urgency, backlog,

organized/disorganized, must be done in the evening/ over the weekend, etc.)

4. Finally, add any additional items you can think of that require your attention or time that I haven't yet mentioned.
5. Now, draw a thick line right below your compliance section (#1 above).

Every item below that line is something you're probably providing at no additional charge. This is how the scope of your client work slowly creeps up on you.

For items listed under #3 on your list, where you consider taking on and pricing work, I suggest you begin following this maxim with your clients when they ask you to address their "urgent" situation:

> ***Your lack of planning does not constitute MY emergency.***

I wouldn't expect my mechanic to open up shop at 9:00 p.m. because my battery died yesterday, and I forgot I had a meeting tomorrow morning. He might, but it would cost me a pretty penny. It's a fee I might be willing to pay if it was that urgent because I don't have the skillset to fix my car.

Your clients don't have your skillset either; otherwise, they wouldn't need you. These factors are also value-adds that you must take into consideration before taking on or quoting a client. I'm going to take you, step-by-step, through #2 above in chapter 6.

Are your wheels turning yet?

Chapter 3

WHAT'S HOLDING YOU BACK?

Almost everyone I speak with in this industry has the same things to say about why they haven't taken any action toward getting out of compliance hell and into the advisor role: "I'm too busy and don't have time." "I don't have anything to offer that's of value." "My client base is different." Or my all-time favourite, "One day, when I'm not so busy, I'll start working **on** my business."

While everyone thinks their issues are unique, I can tell you they are not. In fact, they are almost predictable. That's okay. You're not alone. If you're like most of the experienced bookkeepers I talk to, you have a multitude of reasons you still feel stuck on the hamster wheel.

Now, when you hear about other bookkeepers who've transitioned into advisor roles, I want you to ask—why not me?

POSITIVES AND NEGATIVES

When I'm speaking at an event, I always have the attendees do an exercise right then and there. So, go get a piece of paper and a pen, and let's do this right now (not later!).

STEP 1

Take your piece of paper and fold it in half vertically. On the left side of the paper, write "Negative." On the right side, write "Positive."

STEP 2

Let's start with the negative side. (Yes. I know we all want to be positive but identifying the negative will help you get to the positive!) Write down all the reasons you think you *can't* change the way you run your business and scale it so you can focus on the high-value advisory. Like this:

Negative

- I can't charge more money. I'll lose clients.
- The only way I can make more money is by taking on even more clients.
- I'm already working nights and weekends to keep up.
- I'm so busy; there's no way I have time to scale right now.
- I can't bring on anyone to help me because I don't have time to train or babysit them.
- No one else can do my work the way I do.
- My clients have no idea how much I do for them.
- I can't go on vacation because I'll have twice the work to do when I get back.

- My clients need to reach me, so I have to make myself available.

STEP 3

Now, move to the right column and write down all the amazing things you'd *like* to be able to say about your business in an ideal world, like this:

Positive

- My fees are based on the value I provide.
- My fees have nothing to do with what anyone else is charging.
- I work when I want to work and never outside of the hours I set.
- All the work is organized, and I know exactly what's going on.
- I'm able to delegate to someone.
- My team does the work exactly the same way I do.
- My clients know my value and happily pay for it.
- When I go on vacation or take time off, everything runs smoothly without me.
- I have built a business separate from me; I can sell it or have a revenue stream that's not dependent on me.

My career has prepared me exceptionally well to help you move from the left-hand column to the right. I work with professional bookkeepers and accountants all the time. I'm the go-to person (been there, done that!) when you're ready to make a change. Whatever excuses you've got, bring 'em! It's time to blow that crap up.

I want you to really look at that positive side and picture your life as if everything you wrote down were true right now. Do you think it's impossible? It's not, and I'll show you how to make it a reality.

STOP SELLING YOURSELF SHORT!

Why do we still see ourselves as "just bookkeepers"? That's easy to answer. We think we're "just bookkeepers" because that's what we think we're in business to do. Don't get me wrong. At one point, that's exactly what you did. But now, you have years of experience under your belt. You know things and execute things that you would not have been able to do in your rookie years. It's time to pass the torch and level up.

This is not about multiple degrees in finance. This is not about what "other people" can do. It's about YOU and what you can do with your experience, especially if you build it out correctly with the path I'm laying out in front of you.

Look, I'm no finance guru. I didn't even go into this field intentionally! In 1991, I graduated from college as a certified esthetician. When I opened up my own shop, I didn't want to spend the money on a bookkeeper. Instead, I went to school at night to learn how to do it myself. (Yes, a physical school. There was no online learning then!)

But all I learned was how to complete a set of books. Although my salon failed miserably, I was fortunate to have a lot of salon clients with businesses. I was able to acquire a few of them as bookkeeping clients. Turns out, I really liked bookkeeping and was good at it. I began pursuing that career, slowly adding more and more clients. Eventually, I was able to make a complete career shift.

But, as you know, basic bookkeeping can get boring and overwhelming. It restricts your freedom and doesn't pay enough. I wanted more.

We've all heard of the importance of working "on" your business, not just "in" it. But it's painfully hard to do that without knowing what direction to take.

DON'T MAKE THE MISTAKES I MADE!

> *"You need to spend time ON your business instead of always IN it."*

As my business grew, I knew I had to change the way I was running it, but I had no idea how to get off that hamster wheel. I was the queen of shiny objects! I looked at anything and everything that promised to make things easier for me. My route looked a lot like this when I tried to go from working in my business to working on my business because I had no direction.

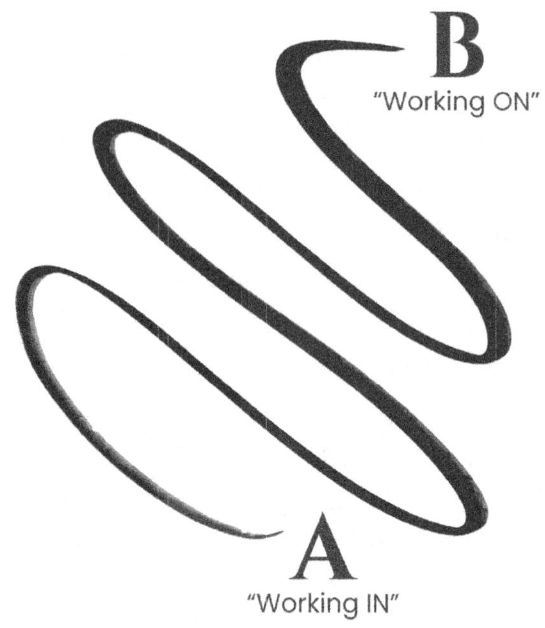

What a time suck! I spent so much time and money trying to get my shit together just to find a way out of overwhelm. Ninety percent of what I tried failed because it was random—no order and no sequence. Frustrating? To say the least.

I want to give you the benefit of what I've learned through all my years of trial and error, so you don't have to repeat my mistakes. That way, you'll be able to go from A to B in a straight line—and in a fraction of the time it took me.

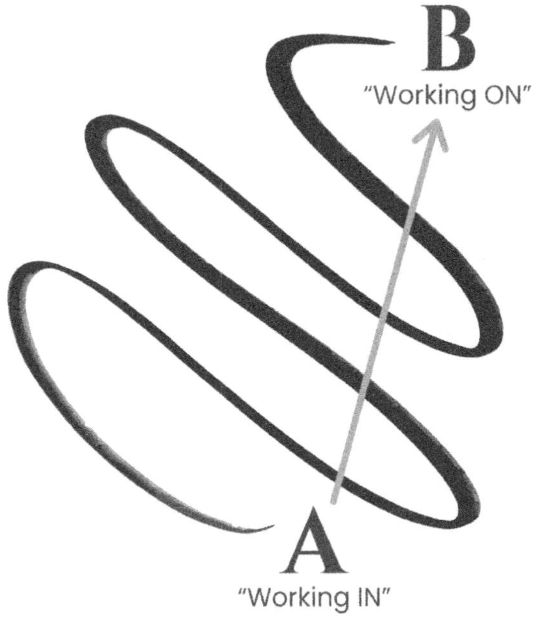

Here's what I want you to understand, know, and believe right now:

> ***The fact that you created a practice that's put you into overwhelm is in itself a huge deal. You should pat yourself on the back for doing it!!!***

YOU got the clients. YOU do a fantastic job. YOU created a living for yourself out of nothing. You didn't settle for a nine-to-five job with benefits. Way to go!

Now, it's time to take what you've already done, re-work it, build on that foundation, and create the life YOU want. You've come this far, all on your own. Why stop now?

Chapter 4

THE SECRET KEY TO TIME, MONEY, AND FREEDOM

I want to work 40 hours per week. I want to take holidays. I want to offer a group coaching program. I want to delegate bookkeeping, tax, and administrative work with confidence that it's being done profitably and with excellence. I want to love my business and not be so overwhelmed.

—ELLEN HUMPHREY-ALLEN, CPA

Ever since you began practicing, you've been bombarded with recommendations and offers for systems, processes, workflow, ideal client selection, and value-based pricing methods that promise to transform your practice.

But there's a disconnect. With these never-ending promises of success, there's no mention of what to do first or what to do next. In fact, many plans begin because we know other people are working on these things, so we figure we'd better work on them too.

We decide to start somewhere and usually end up putting the cart before the horse. We create workflows before we have a system; we develop websites before we know the types of clients we're trying to attract. And soon, we've fallen down a rabbit hole of confusion and frustration.

Insider Tip

I always tell bookkeepers I work with that if they want to learn something, "find someone who's done what you want to do and learn from them." This advice comes from experience.

I once paid a "business coach" a lot of money because she was an "expert." It was one of those nights I was scouring the internet trying to get answers. Suddenly, up popped a "live" webinar (turns out it was evergreen) that seemed to have all the answers. She talked a good game, and I thought this investment was the solution. I was sold on the spot.

Looking back, I realize my error. I had never heard of this woman, and I didn't know what made her an expert. More importantly, she wasn't a bookkeeper. She had no idea where I was coming from and had no clue what I went through on a day-to-day basis (never mind how to get out of it).

What was I thinking???

The result? Work goes by the wayside, and we're still no further ahead than when we started. More likely, we've fallen even more behind.

Do you remember Jennifer from chapter 2? She was in a perpetual struggle to catch up. She couldn't even hire someone to help because she didn't have time to set up systems.

I'm guessing your situation may not be that different from hers. If that's the case, then you're already overwhelmed with compliance work. You're in a never-ending (and futile) race just to keep up (I've been there!), and your time is never your own.

You want to stop working "on the books" and move toward advising clients but wonder how others do it. How have they managed to move away from doing the day-to-day transactional work themselves, so they can focus on advisory work? How are they able to find the right clients at the right fees who want the value they provide? How are THEY able to make so much more money and have so much more time to develop their business?

Their secret? They have the right *systems* in place, so they have full control of everything going on inside their firms. In other words, they have created their *ecosystem.*

THE ECOSYSTEM

Everything that goes on inside your practice is part of an ecosystem—YOUR ecosystem.

From the moment a client or prospect finds you, every interaction they have with your firm must be part of the bigger whole. I call it an ecosystem because each element and action interact with and build off all the others, with each aspect crafted perfectly to produce the end result both you and your clients want.

This will only happen when you create a predictable, measurable process that happens intentionally and systematically for every client—from the moment they appear as a potential lead, throughout the onboarding process, during their regular processing, and finally, when working with you as their advisor.

Imagine your ecosystem as a bubble. Every business owner in the world lives outside that bubble: tire kickers, price shoppers, info seekers, start-ups, multimillion-dollar companies, industries, for-profit, not-for-profit, brick and mortar, online, old school, condescending, micromanagers, philanthropists, hands-off, hands-on, value-seekers, cheapskates.

You want to regulate who comes into that bubble and what happens once they're in. As much as possible, you must automate this process to reduce the time you personally have to spend on it.

You want only the right people coming into your bubble—those who are looking for the solutions you provide.

How many times have you sat on a phone call with a lead that's not at all a good fit for your business? Think of the many times you've had to try to convince a prospect of your value. And how often have you taken on clients whose processes you've had to learn, in an industry you're not familiar with, employing software you don't know how to use? Now, think of all the unbillable hours it took you to get up to speed with every one of those clients!

Creating a hands-*off* way to get ideal clients to come to you who are also willing to pay for the value you offer is not magic. It's intentional.

THE FOUNDATION OF YOUR ECOSYSTEM

To create your ecosystem, you must develop four key aspects of your business.

→ Position Your Value to Attract the Right Clients

Instead of simply listing your services or credentials, your message needs to focus on the biggest *problems* your clients face and how you can help solve them. You should repeatedly emphasize how you are able to help business owners with their business decisions. Every platform needs to send this consistent message—your website, LinkedIn, Facebook, Instagram, and Twitter.

I showed you how to start this shift in chapter 2 with the exercise where you separated compliance work from value-added work. Now that you've separated the two and can clearly identify your own value-adds, we start to build on them. Stick with me here. We'll dive into it in greater detail later in the book.

→ Systemize Everything in Your Firm

Using checklists, instructions, and protocols, every task involved in any client's processing needs to be detailed and recorded. This way, you can delegate this work to someone else on your team, knowing it will be done properly and reliably so that you can do what you've been contracted to do—advise them in their business.

While you'll benefit from systemizing all aspects of your business, the most impactful process you'll create will be one for client intake.

To avoid low-paying (and often PITA!) clients, you can't continue taking on everyone who is willing to pay for your services—no more wasting time on tire-kicking phone calls or with people who can't afford your higher-end offerings.

Instead, create an intake system that filters leads, so you only talk to potential ideal clients. This gives you a systematic way of determining fit, scoping and quoting, contracting, and onboarding.

Ideally, this intake system is part of a well-designed ecosystem and doesn't consume any of your time until someone meets your ideal client criteria. Then, you schedule the discovery call. Up to that point, everything gets handled automatically because you've designed it that way.

If you determine a prospect is a good fit for your firm and they've agreed to your fees, you then funnel them into the system your team uses to process compliance work.

→ Leverage Workflow Software

Ultimately, the systems you implement will only be as good as your ability to monitor and manage them. This can be quite challenging on sticky notes or Excel spreadsheets.

Imagine having the ability to see the status of each client's work—due dates, recurrences, task completion—all on one screen. You can do this by using the glorious invention of cloud-based workflow software.

Placing your systems in a cloud-based workflow will benefit you AND your team (or future team). Basically, everyone logs in each and every time they sit down to work. In front of them is a list of tasks that need to be completed for each client with due dates and priority, and each of these lists contains step-by-step instructions from you about how to do the work.

Expectations are set, instructions are given in detail, timelines are established, and you have the comfort of being able to monitor and manage the work going on inside your firm, with no more double-checking or fixing as you try to stay afloat.

→ Reposition Yourself as an Expert

The final part of creating your ecosystem is establishing where you sit in all of it. You've been at this work for a long time. You've seen all the stories the numbers tell, and you've lived through the battles your clients have faced. It's time to take that experience and put it to good use.

Now that you no longer have to do the compliance work, you have the ability to focus on the value your experience can bring to your clients. Instead of being a necessary expense, you'll become a necessary *partner* in your clients' decision-making process.

Everything you do now is about the problems you solve and the results you provide for your clients. It's no longer just about numbers in, numbers out. The compliance work is still an essential part of the work your company does, but YOU aren't the one doing it—your team is.

The systems you've implemented to manage the compliance work will ensure the numbers you're using are accurate when you create strategies for solving the problems your clients struggle with. With your ecosystem in place, you can reposition yourself as a strategist and expert. You can focus on advising, while your team can focus on the numbers in, numbers out details.

The universal message you will present through your encounters, your website, and your social media will speak to the problems your experience and expertise can help your prospects resolve.

Your intake system will filter all your firm's leads so that discovery calls will only involve prospects who are a good fit for what you offer.

You will no longer trade time for money. You will sell *results,* and your fees will reflect that. And so will your newly recovered personal life, since your time will finally be your own.

Chapter 5

DO THIS FIRST

I know we can't win every client, but it still bugs me that I spent 30 minutes getting to know a potential client only to hear that we're too expensive.

—ANDREW ROYER, ROYER ACCOUNTING

How many times have you hung up the phone from yet another discovery call feeling deflated and like you just wasted another chunk of time you could have spent working?

Do you have a "Free Consultation" or "Complimentary Call" button on your website? Do you answer your phone directly? If you answered yes to either of those questions, you need to read this and take the actions I'm about to show you right away.

In the last chapter, I touched on an intake system. Remember, this is the entrance to your bubble. To create this very crucial part of your ecosystem, you'll need to look at things like who you want to work with, who you won't work with (individual or industry), revenue targets (this is important—you can't take everyone if you want to meet your targets!), which software you'll use, etc. Addressing these points is an essential aspect of creating, perfecting, and then automating your intake system.

Yes, there's definitely some very detailed work that goes into making the intake process ideal in your ecosystem. But I want to show you a few simple things you can do right now to get yours started so you can eliminate some of those tire-kicking, price-shopping, "give me answers for free" phone calls.

THE INTAKE FORM

Before you hang up the phone one more time, thinking to yourself, "If I had known that, I wouldn't have wasted my time on that call!"—do this one simple thing.

Write a list of questions you most commonly ask on a prospective client call.

Focus on things that would be really handy to know before the call, so you don't have to waste time asking and then enduring the long explanations in response. We're going to use this list to give you back some time—keep reading!

You: When was the last time your accounts were reconciled?

Them: Not for almost a year. My bookkeeper got sick and couldn't work anymore and...blah blah blah...then I tried to do them and messed them all up, and then I had *to find another bookkeeper, which was a total disaster... blah blah blah...and then the new bookkeeper I found wanted $3,000 to bring them up to date, but I couldn't afford that so...blah blah blah...*

Wouldn't it just be so much easier if you didn't have to ask? If you already had the (short) answer right in front of you? Let's craft the questions that get you this information before you even talk to a prospect.

First, think of a few simple questions where the prospect's answers or comments are likely to result in a no-sale (e.g., "You're too expensive"). These can be very straightforward, intentional questions like, "What are your annual revenues?" and "What are your total monthly expenses?" If someone has very low revenues, they probably can't afford you yet. If you get their monthly expense amount, you can compare that to annual revenues and see if they're struggling, so you'll know they're price sensitive.

Now, think of client situations you *don't* want to deal with, like, "I have a custom accounting system." If you're exclusively a QuickBooks Online person, a client like this would be a royal pain! "Which accounting software do you use?" is a very simple question to ask and can save you a phone call if you know they use software you have no interest in learning.

Now, take this list of information you'd like to have before a call and create a form. (You can do this by using Google Forms or something similar. All you're trying to do is get some details before scheduling your time.)

Add your logo, pretty up the form, and don't forget to include a place on the form where prospects can add their contact information! Then, grab the URL link to the form and immediately go to your website and change the "Free Consultation" button to include a link to this form.

WHAT TO DO WITH THIS MAGICAL LITTLE FORM

Do leads randomly email you because they saw your info somewhere? Do your friends and family give out your email to anyone who needs a bookkeeper because they think they're doing you a favour? Okay, let's fix that problem right now. Draft a generic email in which you'll write something wonderful, like:

> *Thank you for contacting us! At ABC Company, we strive to be of the utmost service to our clients. It would really help us to help you if you would take a moment to complete our questionnaire (insert the link to your form) before we get on a call. Thank you so much, and we'll be in touch with the next steps as soon as we receive your responses.*

Once you have the draft email the way you want it, save it as a template. The next time you get an inquiry by email, pull up the template, add the person's name, and hit send. That's it.

Are you still answering the phone the old-fashioned way? Stop that. Seriously. My phone number isn't published on any of my websites or lead systems (like QuickBooks Online "Find an Accountant"). Nope. The only way to get to me is through my intake form. Go change your outgoing phone message right now. Make it similar to the email you created and direct prospects to your website's "Complimentary Call" button. Now, don't answer the phone unless you know who it is!

FORM RESPONSES = POWER FOR YOU

Once you have this form for your leads to complete in advance, you're way ahead of the game going into a call—or NOT going into a call. That's the point.

If you craft your questions carefully, you'll get enough information in the responses to decide whether or not you even want to talk with this person. If the responses indicate they're probably not a good fit for you, why would you want to spend time on a discovery call? I hope you just muttered, "I wouldn't want to." So use what's in front of you to make a choice, and you'll have more control over your time.

> ***I don't have to do anything until the prospect has already made the discovery call appointment on my calendar. I can't imagine going back to the way I used to do things.***
>
> —SARAH FACIO-DAVIS, ACCURATE OFFICE HELP

GOOD FIT OR NO FIT—WHAT TO DO WITH EACH

Create two email templates.

TEMPLATE 1

The first email template is what you send to the prospects you WANT to speak with, based on their answers. It will contain a link to your schedule and ask the prospect to select a time that works for them. Close the email with something like, "I look forward to speaking with you," or whatever sounds more like you.

TEMPLATE 2

You'll send the second email template to prospects who are NOT a good fit. Thank them for completing the form and then add something like, "At this time, we're probably not a good fit for you," and then provide them with some other options. For example, do you have someone you can refer them to? Can you provide a link to an industry membership organization where they can post an opportunity? Do you have any DIY digital assets you could link to? We always want to be of service, so it's important to send them off in a positive, helpful way.

Using the intake form and your email templates, you've now created a system that makes it easier to be selective about the leads you choose to work with moving forward. This simple little system, which you can create immediately, will save you from those dreaded dead-end calls you wish you'd never had.

Chapter 6
HOW TO GET OUT OF YOUR OWN WAY

For me, one of the most rewarding things about taking bookkeepers through this process is watching their transformation—when they get to that moment where they actually see for themselves what they can create, based on the skills and experience they already have.

I get it. I know how they feel. I remember when things started coming together for my business, and I thought, "Holy crap. I'm actually creating something meaningful, something that matters to my clients. They don't see me as just their bookkeeper anymore!"

Suzanne is a perfect example of this. I love working with her, and the story of how she has been able to grow her business by creating her company's ecosystem—and then specializing as an advisor—is both exciting and inspirational.

But don't take my word for it. Listen to how Suzanne describes the struggles and triumphs of her journey in her own words:

> *Before I started working with Lisa, I had already built a solid business. My years of hard work had paid off, and I always thought it was amazing that I had come this far by getting to do something I loved.*
>
> *But when I turned 40 last year, I started asking myself, "Is this what you want to keep doing for the next 20 years?"*
>
> *My goal, for so long, had been to make as much money as I could, to build the business, and to be comfortable. But now that I had accomplished those things, I felt like I needed a new goal—something that I really cared about. I had built the platform, but what was I going to say when I stood up on it?*
>
> *I began reading about a lot of new programs and strategies and started trying to implement those, just to make this "better." But all these attempts meant I was working even harder. And everything became just too much—too much work and too many options.*
>
> *I didn't know where to focus my time. I was doing a lot of things well, but I wasn't doing anything great—because I wasn't saying no to anything.*
>
> *Because I wasn't feeling productive, my workday was never really done, and it was later and later before I could tell myself, "Okay, now I can go engage my family." I was missing out on time with my husband and my four kids.*

I felt like I was just spinning—that everything was a little bit out of control.

I remembered when I was starting out, grinding away at jobs I didn't like. I would wake up in the morning dreading to go to work. Once I was there, I'd stare at the clock and think, "It's only two o'clock?" I had promised myself I would never go back to that.

But now, I was doing that and feeling that again. I had too much work, and I just didn't want to do any of it. And I thought, "The point of this is to enjoy it, right?"

Money alone wouldn't be enough to move me towards something better. I needed something true, something I could be great at and known for.

The tipping point came when I was asked to speak at a conference. I heard lots of the other speakers say they were doing some great thing, or had standardized their operation in some powerful way, or had achieved great success by specializing. And all I could say was, "Crap. I'm not anywhere I should be."

To get where I wanted to be, I needed to specialize and become an advisor. I obviously wasn't going to get to that level on my own, and I needed to find someone and something that made sense to me. That's when I joined Lisa's mastermind group.

THE DESIRE TO CHANGE

Most of the people I work with begin with the desire to change the way they operate but have no idea how to do it. Their trepidation, mixed with excitement, is almost palpable.

They've been working the grind for so long that they've lost sight of all the little things that have been accumulating in their brains. All the things they instinctively know how to do—the processes or solutions they've come up with for their clients, and how they've guided them through different situations that come up.

As soon as Suzanne took the plunge and committed to becoming an advisor, all her doubts and fears came to the surface.

> *When I first began the program, I was very skeptical. I was born skeptical and doubting, so I didn't know if this was a good move or not.*
>
> *I also hate doing something because everyone else is doing it. I think too many people are followers. I don't want to be one of the masses. I like to tell myself, "You're too special for that." It's a great excuse for not taking a risk, isn't it?*
>
> *You know how bookkeepers often don't value themselves, so they don't try to scale up?*
>
> *My problem is the opposite.*
>
> *I don't like being one of the many. And I don't want to follow something just because someone told me to. I need to do things for myself. (Definitely the hard way to create any valuable change.) I'd say I had a good deal of resistance when I joined Lisa's program.*
>
> *But I had to do the work. I was paying good money for this program, so if I didn't give it a chance, it meant I was just kidding myself about wanting to systemize and expand.*

> *My husband has always been very supportive, so he was completely behind me and the investment of time and money. But knowing me as he does, he also added, "Just make sure it's worth it. Go in and do what you're told, and don't argue about it the whole time."*

The first step on Suzanne's transformation was to take a hard look at her company's ecosystem—how everything fit together, whether her team was following consistent processes, and where Suzanne's place was in all of this. We knew she'd never be able to grow her business if she couldn't hand over some of her responsibilities to the members of her team (especially the tasks she hated doing).

> *I finally followed my husband's advice! I let go of my attachment to doing everything my way and trying to control everything and dove into Lisa's approach.*
>
> *And it worked!*
>
> *It was amazing to see the results for my company and me. As we systemized, work became easier and more focused, clients we wanted to work with appeared, and my stress started to lessen.*
>
> *As we began transforming our systems and processes, the biggest shift was probably felt by my staff. As we began to develop our ecosystem, I repeatedly encountered situations where half my staff had been doing something one way, and the other half did it differently. That's when I got serious about creating standard operating procedures for everything we did across all of our clients.*

At first, it was a ton of work. We had to figure out systems, put everything in place, and then write it all down. It had to be communicated to the team, and then we had to follow up to make sure everyone was conforming to the systems in the same way.

This was, by far, the hardest part for me. I had always been more of a big-picture person, while most bookkeepers are super detail-oriented. Forcing myself to sit down and write out SOPs without skipping large steps was not easy. In the past, my team would tell me that when I gave them a written procedure, it often had way too many holes in it. This time had to be different. I took their comments and worked at plugging those holes.

As soon as the systems fell into place, I saw the real value in this approach. I become a lot more open to everyone's processes, and I realized that everything didn't have to be done my way. My team is amazing. Since team members often have great ideas for improving something, we created a forum where we can discuss an idea and then update the SOP. Everyone on the team implements that improvement. We can now leverage the expertise of each member of our team.

Once I made that leap, I was able to promote one of my team members to a managerial level. She took over the things I don't like to do, freeing me to do a lot more of what I wanted to do to grow the company. (A part of me would still like to know everything, but now I know I simply can't.)

In addition to gaining more time and more revenue, another huge benefit of having our ecosystem in place is

> *how we all feel about our jobs. Everyone in my company now follows the same principles and procedures, so the playing field is levelled. We're more of a real team.*
>
> *There's no worry or resentment. There are no feelings of "She doesn't have to do that, but I do," because all of us are doing the same thing. If one of our bookkeepers is more experienced or a lot better than another bookkeeper because of his or her natural strengths and talents, the others get to benefit. When one of them knows or learns a new process, that person can share it and help others employ it as well.*
>
> *Staff evaluations have also become much easier and more effective. Prior to Lisa's mastermind, I evaluated everyone based on what I knew about the way each one did things. With that approach, I never could have brought on a manager because there was no standard for evaluating everyone equitably. Failing to systemize had actually stopped me from scaling my business.*
>
> *Now, I was ready to move forward.*

When our systems are in place, we are free to devote a lot more of our energy into designing what we want our business to be. Discovering how we can become advisors for the clients we truly want to work with by specializing in particular skills and areas.

When we actually look at what we do in detail, we begin to see things we were oblivious to all along. When was the last time you analyzed your clients' businesses, looking for commonalities and looking at special processes or spreadsheets you created specifically for them?

Right out of the gate, Suzanne and I worked on her compliance work systems. "You need a system to attract the clients who will benefit from your passion for helping," I told her. "But first, we need to get the bookkeeping looked after, so you can focus on this."

Establishing systems across her company would free her up to really hone in on how she could advise her clients and fulfill her dream of doing what she loved to do.

While the systems were being set up, we started looking at her long-term goals—how she wanted to serve and what she could do with her existing knowledge and experience. So now, let's do the same thing for you.

EXPANDING YOUR VALUE

You already identified your value in chapter 2. Now let's go through each of those value-add items you listed and see how you can expand on those.

For example, if you regularly provide cash flow planning for your existing clients, you're probably quite good at it. Maybe you offer this service to many clients within the same industry. Now, you need to build on that situation.

Let's say you have a number of clients who are dentists, and you regularly offer them your cash flow expertise. Not only that, every month, you also spend an hour reviewing and planning your forecast with each of them. Additionally, you make yourself available to help them understand how to adjust their plans for unforeseen circumstances. Add to this the fact that you do this so often and with so many clients that you've been able to identify patterns across multiple dentists. You share your knowledge of these patterns freely with your clients, and they're able to make decisions based on what you've shared.

In other words, you have inadvertently become a strategic cash flow planning specialist for dentists. So leverage that! Position yourself as that expert. Promote yourself as such, *in addition to* the superior bookkeeping work being done by YOUR firm under your supervision.

BREAK IT DOWN

You can do this sort of breakdown with any industry and any of the items you wrote below the compliance line in chapter 2. Just look for small clusters of similar clients.

Maybe you have a lot of nonprofits. You know that the reporting and grant applications/reconciliations you do for them are not standard stuff. They require specific knowledge and precise accounting. Or perhaps you have multiple restaurants, contractors, real estate agents, lawyers, etc. Each of those industries has its own special requirements, so build on what you're already doing.

Working with Suzanne, our goal was to get her to see if there was anything right in front of her that she wasn't seeing. When Suzanne broke down everything she and her team were doing for her clients, there it was! She had a couple of churches as clients, and they loved her work. Churches have very specific requirements when it comes to bookkeeping. Even more important, just from working with these particular clients, Suzanne knew things the average bookkeeper wouldn't.

We expanded on what she knew. She built her value promise up so that she could speak to the unique problems that churches face and become their solution to solving those problems.

But wait, it gets better! Because Suzanne knew the industry and was able to speak their language (if you haven't read it yet, Jeffrey Shaw's *Lingo* was how I learned how to speak my clients' "language"), she was able to position her offering at the district level. She created a high-value package that the district promoted to their churches and would send directly to Suzanne's firm.

Thanks to positioning herself this way, she describes her experience with one of those churches:

> *I was referred by the district to a new church that was opening. I met with the new pastor, who told me the concerns they were facing, like how to know what kind of people they should hire and what kinds of skills would be useful. I offered to lay all that out for him and told him that these were the kinds of things we specialized in.*
>
> *When we finished and I had given him lots of ideas about how he could overcome some of the challenges he faced, he asked, "Can I pray with you?"*
>
> *I said sure, and afterward, he said, "I just want you to know that you're now part of our family. You're such a teacher!" I was close to tears as I thought to myself, "My doctor clients never pray with me. This is the most rewarding thing I've ever done."*

Moments like these are so rewarding because they show me the work I can do as an advisor. It means something. It's a different win than just getting a paycheque. It's about having a bigger purpose.

Needless to say, I no longer watch the clock with dread. I no longer hate the thought of going to work. And I give my family lots of time and attention.

I love what I do. I love my team, and we love the clients we work with. I can do more of the things that I really want to do, knowing that my clients, whom I really care about, will always get great service.

And none of this would be true if I hadn't decided to take this journey.

If you're reading this and are hesitant like I was, I would encourage you to take the leap and specialize. You'll have more revenue, more sanity, more freedom, more purpose, and higher standing. And you'll have made the job fun again.

YOU HAVE IT IN YOU, NOW FIND IT

It might be that you have just one client who has something unique that you understand deeply. I want to make this clear: YOU have an understanding of it, not every other bookkeeper. This is your opportunity to expand on that.

It's not about being a genius—it's about embracing what you know that others don't. What experience you have that others want. Every industry has something unique that you can specialize in.

I guarantee that if I were to look at your processes, I'd discover a system or an approach that's specific to a problem you solved in an industry you already know. It doesn't have to be big, just different. Start with that, build on it, and voila, you have the beginning of your high-value proposition.

Chapter 7

DO THIS TO TAKE BACK YOUR CALENDAR

How can you possibly find the time to create everything you need to create to make this shift when you're already buried under a mountain of compliance work and backlog? The real question is, *how can you not*?

Quite often, when something seems daunting or intimidating, we put it on the lowest priority level of our to-do list, saying, "When things slow down, I'll do it," or "As soon as I hire someone, I can start working on this."

These statements themselves are natural, yet they're looking at things backwards. When you put the time in, things WILL start to slow down for you. Putting the time in is what gets you to a position where you can hire in a way that won't jeopardize your operation.

Time is the number one obstacle everyone I speak with faces. I get it. I didn't have time either. Or so I thought.

We all have the same 24 hours in a day. It's what we do with these hours that makes the difference. I remember when I was building out my ecosystem; I'd work all day, usually evenings and weekends too. When I finally got through the day, the last thing I wanted to do was work ON my business. Netflix and a glass of wine were so much more appealing.

I would look at all the million and one things I thought I had to implement and think, "Crap. I'm never going to figure this out, never mind get it the way I want it." I was so focused on the big picture that I couldn't find my way to get any momentum going.

> ***Stop looking at the whole ladder and focus on one rung at a time instead.***
>
> —MICHAEL PALMER, CO-FOUNDER, PURE BOOKKEEPING

My coach at the time, Michael Palmer, author and podcast host of *The Successful Bookkeeper*, gave me my first aha moment. "Break it down," he said.

So, I looked at how I could break down the big picture into smaller, actionable steps and focused on getting things done "one rung at a time." I realized that every objective could be whittled down into smaller, more manageable chunks. Chunking tasks made them much easier to tackle because I was able to move forward and progress slowly, instead of feeling like I wasn't accomplishing anything.

But for me, time was still an issue. Yes, the tasks seemed more doable, but where was I going to find the time to complete them? That's when I learned about time blocking.

TIME BLOCKING

Time blocking is the process of intentionally creating blocks of time to get things done. It literally saved my ass.

> *Time blocking made me more aware of time wasted and made me feel more productive in my day.*
> —SUSAN NORTHEY,
> ACCURATE ACCOUNTING & TAX SERVICE

I used to sit down at my desk, plow through as much work as I could, run to make dinner, go back to work, then give the kids a bath, get them to bed, and hope for enough energy and motivation at the end of the day to work on my business, doing the "chunks." I'll bet you can imagine how that went and how often I actually made any progress.

Using a Google search, I found all sorts of techniques for blocking time. I was able to create blocks of time on my calendar for everything I intended and needed to do. That included things like client work, admin stuff, lunch, invoicing, and business development.

With time blocking, I started to organize my schedule like a school day: Period 1 —client work, Period 2 —admin work, Period 3...you get the idea. The trick is to treat it like you actually have to get up and move to the next class whenever you come to the end of a block.

Creating time blocks in this way did a few things for me. First, I didn't get lost in one client's work, leaving the rest to fall behind. Instead, I took everything that needed to be done in a week and split it out into reasonable blocks of time. Second, it gave me specific appointments *with myself* to work on what I needed to do to improve my business and create my ecosystem.

CREATE YOUR BLOCKS

If you do nothing else that I teach in this book, do this. The only way you'll ever find time to work on your business is if you block it out intentionally. Honestly, it's a game-changer.

> ***Now that Lisa has taught me time blocking, I have fewer disruptions because I have times when I'll return emails and calls. This helps me stay focused, be more productive and disciplined.***
> —SHEILA DOWNEY, INSYTE BUSINESS SOLUTIONS

This isn't something you need to spend all day on. You can get started very easily and quickly. But DO NOT fill every open gap of time with client work!

I was so excited to try time blocking that I missed a very important detail. I set up all of my blocks, feeling super accomplished that I was now in control of my time. But I literally filled every minute of every day with something. There was no room to move anything anywhere or see when I had the capacity for something else!

Instead, choose specific increments of time each day that you'll dedicate to client work. This will show you where you have the capacity for more work. (I know, right now you're thinking there's no way you can take on more work! So just time block for a few weeks and see what happens!)

I also urge you to go to your calendar right now, while you have this section in front of you, and get started blocking.

I'll help you do it:

1. Decide how much time you WANT to dedicate to improving, restructuring, and growing your business each week (One hour? Two hours?).
2. Decide which day(s) and time(s) of the week you think would be best to do it.
3. Now, put it in your calendar and label it "Business Development." Make it a nice bright colour and make it recurring—indefinitely.
4. Now, block 30 minutes a day to stand up, walk around, and eat lunch (we all tend to skip this important part of our day!). Make this a different colour and recurring indefinitely as well.
5. Create a block for checking emails and social media—set a recurrence daily.
6. Create another block for your billing and administrative tasks. This is usually once or twice per month. Keep going with the protocol of colour and recurrence.
7. Create blocks for client work. These can be general or specific for each client.
8. Add any other regular items you need to get done as blocks on your calendar in the same format.

Bonus Tip: I like to set my calendar to give me a 10- [illegible] warning when the next block is about to start. This [illegible] the ability to wind down what I'm doing, knowing [illegible] focus on something else in the next block.

THE 30-DAY CHALLENGE

The thing about time blocking is that no one can really understand how powerful it is until they actually do it. "I know I need to time block. I just have to find time to do it." We just walked through it in a matter of minutes. Doesn't that statement seem a little ridiculous now? I'm always amazed at how people put off doing such a simple exercise that produces incredible, freeing results.

> ***Scheduling used to take a ridiculous amount of time, but now it's a no-brainer because there is always a block for whatever comes up.***
> —RAE GAGNON, BLUE JEAN BUSINESS SOLUTIONS

Rae hit the time blocking exercise right out of the gate without hesitation. Seriously, it doesn't take long, and the results are immediate.

Now that you've just created your time blocks, you need to stick to them. Religiously. So I invite you to a 30-day time blocking challenge. Starting tomorrow, make it your top priority to adhere to your time blocks for one entire month. Treat each block as sacred. Trust me—it will pay off.

Hold yourself accountable! Send me an email (Lisa@LisaCampbellProfitCoach.com) with the subject line "30-Day Time Block Challenge." If you stick to your blocks, in no time at all, you'll stop the busywork, focus on the real work, and you'll actually get things done. Just the act of setting your intention will make a huge difference.

Chapter 8

TRICKS TO HAVING ONLY IDEAL, HIGH-TICKET CLIENTS

We all have those PITA clients we wish we could fire, but we keep holding on to them. Getting to the point where you can pick and choose your clients is extremely liberating, and it's where every bookkeeper should be.

The truth is, you don't have to work with anyone who devalues you, insults you, or doesn't pay you—EVER. It's YOUR business. Yes, I know, "*But Lisa, I need the money.*" So did I.

Karen (not her real name) would text me incessantly—at all hours of the day. Everything was an emergency to her. It was quite normal for me to hear the ding, ding, ding of my text messages at 11:00 p.m. "Urgent: pull from this LOC to pay that credit card, immediately!" or "Urgent: lender needs financial info tomorrow morning." or "Urgent: I want to send my daughter $5K before the morning."

What she was doing was insane. She was so over-leveraged that it was a constant juggling act. She continued to buy properties and shop for high-end items to furnish them, and she couldn't afford any of it. Every credit card and line of credit was maxed out, and somehow, I became the one doing the money transfer dance every day to make sure her minimum payments were met.

She'd tell me, "I know what I'm doing. You just need to keep track of all of it." That's how she saw me—as "just her bookkeeper."

I was constantly asking myself, "Why am I still working with her?" But I knew the answer. She was paying me $60,000 a year, and I couldn't give that up.

I stuck it out with Karen for years. Over time, she began sharing her personal life struggles, and we would end up on the phone sometimes for over an hour while I listened to her bitch about her boyfriend, her kids, her ex, etc. I would roll my eyes, listen, and work at the same time. It got to the point where I would cringe when I saw her name come up on my phone. Something had to change. I couldn't deal with the insults and invasion of my personal time any longer, no matter what the cost would be to my finances.

I had always heard that if you love what you do, it never seems like work. I wanted that! I almost had it, with the exception of Karen.

Almost every bookkeeper I've ever worked with has been in a similar situation more than once. But imagine what your life would look like if every day, you were only working with your ideal clients, who appreciate what you do? What if you never had to experience the "dreaded client" work, phone calls, etc. What if you never had to chase a payment again?

Earlier that year, I had gone through a process of evaluating the clients I had to make sure I was working with people who were in alignment with my core values and who I actually wanted to serve. It was quite an eye-opener, and I strongly encourage you to do it too. Here's what I did.

THE EXISTING CLIENT ANALYSIS

1. Create a spreadsheet. Here's a download that will help you with this: http://lisacampbellprofitcoach.com/client-rating. In the first column, list your clients in order from highest revenue to lowest revenue.
2. Across the top, create columns for the following categories and whatever else matters to you. These are just examples:
   a. Tech savviness
   b. Owner involvement
   c. Pays your invoices promptly
   d. Sends requested documents
   e. Appreciates you
   f. Refers you to others
   g. Nice person
   h. Communicates

3. Now, give each client listed in the first column points ranging from 1 to 10, based on how they measure up to behaviours a) through h) listed above. The better they are at exhibiting each behaviour, the higher the number they get in that column.
4. Now, total the points for each client.
5. Finally, give each client a rating, A, B, C, or D, using your 1-10 totals.

- **61–80 points: A—Awesome Client.** They refer you to others, pay your invoices, appreciate you, and are a great client overall.

- **41–60 points: B—Great Client.** They pay your invoices and appreciate you but don't refer you.
- **21–40 points: C—Not-So-Great Client.** They don't get you documents on time, pay late, argue charges, don't appreciate what you do, and don't refer.
- **20 points or less: D—PITA Client.** They complain all the time, don't appreciate you, devalue what you do, cancel or don't show up for meetings, and basically are time and energy suckers.

TAKE CONTROL OF WHAT YOU DISCOVER

You'll find what you learn to be very valuable. Here's what you do with the information in front of you:

- Seriously move towards firing your D clients. You don't owe them anything, and they're draining you of energy you could apply to your good clients.

- Look at your C clients and see what you could do to move them towards becoming B clients (or As!). Have a conversation with them about where they fall short but position it so that it benefits them. For instance, you could say, "I know it's hard to stay on top of getting me everything I need quickly. I'd like to set you up on an app (e.g., Receipt Bank, Hubdoc, etc.) so that all you have to do is snap a picture with your phone. I'm also putting all my clients on pre-authorized debit, so they don't have to remember to pay me on time. I'll send you the form later on today."
- Call your B clients and ask them to refer you! They may not even be aware this is something you'd like them to do.

Shit. Karen was a D client but was at the top of the list in revenues. I couldn't walk away from that!

I struggled for a long time with this one. I had fired all my D clients and moved my Cs to A or B status. I was only working with my ideal clients—except for Karen. And now, it was blatantly obvious how poorly she fit into my "ideal" model, making it even more miserable to have to work with her every day.

THE TIP THAT SAVED ME

Walt, my "even-better-than-a-husband," was probably more tired of hearing my struggles with her than I was of working with her. His idea of setting a goal (to replace her income) within a defined period of time made perfect sense. This was no longer some abstract "one day" thought of being free of her. It was about to become a reality.

> ***Set a deadline, put it up on the wall, and count it down every month.***
> —WALTER CIMINI

I decided on 12 months. Over the next year, I would focus on attracting enough ideal clients to replace the $60K per year I'd lose once I fired Karen.

I wrote the number 12 on a piece of paper and stuck it to the wall in front of my computer. Every month, I'd cross it out and write a new number: 11, 10, 9, etc. During the countdown, every time she stressed me out, I'd look at that number. It was a great coping mechanism!

I never made it to the number 12! By the time the countdown got to three months left, I'd had enough. I had not yet replaced her income, but the PITA factor was unbearable. I sent Karen a disengagement letter giving her 75 days' notice to replace us. She did not take it seriously and didn't even look for a replacement until the last week we were to stop providing services! It wasn't easy nor amicable, but in the end, it needed to be done.

If you have a Karen or two, please use this method. At the time of this writing, I'm 14 months Karen-free, and business is better than ever. It's amazing what opens up when you recognize your own value and release the time and energy suckers from your life. You know the saying, "When one door closes, another one opens." Open the doors for the clients you want to work with!

Chapter 9

ACCELERATE YOUR BUSINESS BY MOVING BEYOND BOOKKEEPING

If you're still reading this book, I know you don't want to stay in the same spot, doing what you're doing. You want more. More for you, more for your clients.

When I think back to where I was, knowing that change was necessary but not really knowing where I was going, I wish I could encourage my earlier self. Let myself know that I was on the right track, and it would pay off in the end if I just kept going.

There were times I wanted to give up. Just deal with what I had already built and leave it at that. But I knew if I didn't take action to change, I'd still be dealing with the same issues, the same ex-husband, and the same limitations.

I had no way of knowing that what I was creating would transform my life the way it has. Not all the changes were intentional. Some were just really awesome side effects of moving beyond "just bookkeeping" with an ecosystem designed to be in alignment with my values and my goals.

THE LIFE YOU WANT TO CREATE

When you move beyond bookkeeping, your business benefits. But those changes also pay dividends in your life in general. Here are some things I NEVER have to deal with now:

- PITA clients
- Wasted time on phone calls that go nowhere
- "Urgent" client needs
- Trying to get new, ideal clients (they now find *me*)
- Clocking my time
- Justifying my invoices
- Chasing payments
- Working nights or weekends
- Working on vacation
- Compliance work
- Battling a backlog
- Feeling devalued
- Burning out

I literally start each and every day saying, "What am I going to create today, and who am I going to help?"

My day starts when I say it starts. And because I've set up my time blocks, I have scheduled time to be productive and also time to allow for me to take a break/day off/vacation when I want to.

My clients show up to (and actually look forward to!) each and every meeting we set. We have productive discussions where they're actually leaning on me to advise them on whatever the issue at hand is. We work on strategy and implementation, with me as their accountability partner and guide.

Both the client and I walk away from these meetings with a sense of purpose and direction. It is an incredible feeling to know that I'm actually making a positive change in someone's life. What we work on in their business transcends into their personal lives. If the business is successful, it supports a successful home life and personal goals.

When I first met Erin, she had just taken on $140K worth of debt because her studio was drowning. She didn't understand her numbers and was struggling to keep her dream of entrepreneurship afloat.

Her bookkeeper worked in the usual once-a-month processing style, so all Erin ever got to see was what had already happened (and well after the fact). Sure, she looked at her Income Statement and her Balance Sheet, but she didn't really understand them. Even more importantly, no one was helping her use them to run her business.

I ran an assessment of what had gone on in her business over the last several years and was immediately able to see why she had to borrow the $140K. It was blatantly obvious—her business couldn't sustain the model she was operating with. Had we not worked together, she would have had to borrow more money, or even worse, close her doors permanently.

I want to make something very clear here: I don't have a degree in finance. The assessment is not rocket science. It involves simply applying my knowledge and experience (with some additional Profit First training). I then put that understanding to use in a way that helps clients. I say this because you may be thinking, "I don't know how to do that." But you can develop additional skills, in short bursts of time, for whatever you want to add to your already identified value-adds. Never stop learning!

Erin and I have worked together for just over a year now. We meet on Zoom every month, and I keep an eye on things in the background (is she doing what I advised her to do?). At the time of this writing, the world is living in the COVID-19 pandemic and has been for over eight months. Erin had to close her doors temporarily and shift to an online platform. Even with sales down over 50 percent, we were able to move her from a $90K net loss to a $90K net profit in just over a year. How rewarding is that?

MAKING A DIFFERENCE

Think for a moment about your business and the way it is now versus the way it could be. Do you have a lot of satisfaction in your work? Do you look forward to working every day? Do you wish you could create change for your clients in a way that matters to them and to you?

Having spoken with hundreds of bookkeepers over the years, I know there's a lot of overwhelm and self-doubt that stops many from moving forward, so I cannot stress these three facts enough:

1. There is a way off the hamster wheel. More time, money, and freedom await you.
2. It is bookkeepers like you, with the experience you have, who must step up and serve your clients in a desperately needed way.
3. The transition to advisor is not going to happen by itself. If you don't take action now, you'll fall behind and remain an expense to your clients rather than an investment.

> *I am now finally and consistently paying myself first. I go past data entry and compliance by providing my clients with a financial ecosystem. Profit First is just one of the tools I use to help point them in the right direction of running a profitable, sustainable business.*
>
> —JENNIFER HUME, CBTS INC.

Chapter 10
WHAT NEXT?

As I finish this book, I'm thinking about what my day was like yesterday. I woke up at 7:00 a.m., crawled back into bed with my coffee and my journals (as I do every morning), and reflected on the day before. I always document the things that are going right in my life (thank you, Jeffrey Shaw, *Lingo*, for the What's Working Journal idea). I've found this to be an invaluable practice as I proceed along my entrepreneurial journey, recognizing the efforts that have paid off.

I have another journal I write in each day that contains my thoughts on what's going on at the time. Looking back to what I wrote years ago, there's all sorts of stuff in there about my ex and the horrors that followed when I finally left him as well as thoughts about my struggle to scale my business, my clients from hell, etc. What a difference from today. I'm still amazed that I was able to push through to change my circumstances and my business.

Going from the weight of the world being solely on my shoulders to having my entire ecosystem designed to support me and my dreams is a transformation I'm really proud of. I now know that each day, I'm working with my ideal clients, building relationships on trust and results, and building the culture of my team to empower them to achieve their goals as well.

My kids have often asked me, "If you could go back in time and change anything in your life, would you?" The answer is an absolute NO. What I learned from pushing through, fighting my way to where I want to be, is invaluable. You'll be amazed at what you can accomplish if you set your mind to it. My hope for you is that this book makes it easier for you to believe in yourself, put the work in, and create the life you love.

Is your head spinning with ideas? If you're anything like me, you've already started to build out everything you want to do in your head. You know it all makes sense, and you know that if you apply what we're doing here, you'll have a business you love.

YOUR ADVANTAGE

You have a map now—a blueprint that will make this much-needed transition a reality. No more guessing what to work on to level up your business and change your reality.

I've shown you exactly what needs to be done, from my own experience, so you can skip all the mistakes I made along the way and can get right to the good stuff that actually gets results.

Following the recommendations in this book gives you a massive advantage. You've now got the tools you need to get started.

TAKE ACTION NOW!

How many books have you read where you've thought, "That's great. I should do that," and then put the book down and got lost in your work again without ever having implemented what you read?

Not this time. It's right in front of you! You know these are not random tidbits of information designed to inspire every business owner. These are specific action items for YOU—the experienced bookkeeper who's had enough of the grind and is ready to do more.

The whole process doesn't have to be done in a day. Remember, one rung of the ladder at a time.

Remember, this is not just about you and your business. It's about the entrepreneurs you serve too. They need you to help them. Set yourself up for success the way I've shown you. The clock is ticking...

There is never a "right time." There will always be something that will get in your way. It might take six months or even a year. But that time will pass by whatever you do, so think ahead—if you walk away from this book and do nothing, you'll still be in the same place you are right now in six months, a year, five years. Does that sit well with you? Of course not. Make yourself and your business a priority.

If you can block time, you can do this. Go.

THANK YOU

Putting thoughts to paper and publishing a book is an amazing undertaking that I'm proud to have accomplished. It's something I used to think "other people" did, and I never dreamed that I would someday see a book with my own name under the title.

The fact is this book would not have come to fruition without the incredible people I am fortunate enough to have in my life. These are the "other people" who have made this book possible—the ones who believe in me and my message and for whom I am truly grateful.

I am surrounded by such an abundance of inspiring, loving, and supporting friends, family, and associates that it's hard to know where to begin. So, I'll start by thanking Nicole Gebhardt, the founder and genius behind Niche Pressworks. Nicole, without your guidance, I wouldn't have even started this project, let alone finished it!

And to all the others on the Niche Pressworks team whose hard work you're looking at right now: my wonderfully creative and supportive project manager, Kim Han; my editing team, Julie Salzmann and Anna Flynn; my proofreader, Nadia Bechler; and my book designers—thank you. Thank you also to Niche Pressworks for introducing me to Michael Hauge and incorporating his coaching into your strategic book-writing process.

I could never express enough gratitude to Michael Hauge, story expert, consultant (he's worked with Will Smith!!!!), speaker, and author of *Storytelling Made Easy*. His coaching showed me how to express what I wanted to say through stories that readers will actually want to read. Michael, your guidance and knowledge, and your passion for storytelling are incredible. I am honoured to know you and call you my friend.

Of course, I owe much thanks to my photographer, Kathy Spence at Spence Portraits; she's created amazing images to help me build my brand, including the one you see on this book's cover.

Thank you to the phenomenal professionals and experts in this industry who provided their stories and testimonials and granted me the privilege of sharing their experiences with my readers.

Much appreciation and thanks are due to Mike Michalowicz, author of *Profit First* and co-founder of Profit First Professionals, and to my guide, mentor, and all-around cheerleader Ron Saharyan, co-founder of Profit First Professionals. Thanks to both of you for creating such an incredible solution for entrepreneurs and for those of us in the industry who strive to serve them. I am grateful for the trust, respect, and confidence you have in me to lead Profit First Professionals for all of Canada.

My deepest gratitude goes to Michael Palmer, author of *The Successful Bookkeeper*, host of "The Successful Bookkeeper" podcast, CEO of Pure Bookkeeping, and my very first business coach. Michael, without your inspiration, guidance, encouragement, sharing, knowledge, and support, I probably would never have climbed up that ladder rung-by-rung and would still be stuck on the hamster wheel where I started. I also owe you a huge thank you for helping me to believe that I could help others in this industry follow my path and create their dreams. It was your faith in me that empowered me to create my Accelerate 2 Advisor mentorship program. (And a huge thank you as well to Jim Flauaus, founder and president of Anchor Tax Relief, for coming up with the name for that program!).

Thank you to my mindset coach, Kelly Ruta of Becoming Limitless, for blowing up the BS in my head, so I'm now freely able to share my story with you and help you along your own journey.

Thanks as well to Kelly Roach, CEO of The Unstoppable Entrepreneur. Because of her brilliant coaching, I've been able to get my message out to those who need it in a way that makes sense...and it isn't incredibly dry and boring!

To my incredible team, Alex MacFarlane, Corinne Blagg, Janet Mercredi, Jennifer Hume, Sarah Facio-Davis, Jos Willard, Debra Angilletta, and Steve Kushman: Your passion for what you do makes you such an integral part of my mission. For your part in what we're creating, I am truly grateful.

Very special thanks to my sister Renee, my aunt Colleen, and my mom Sharon. We are The Foundational Four—always there for each other. Without your support through the pain of leaving my marriage and the never-ending drama that has been its aftermath, my business and my life would have been a completely different story. I'm forever grateful for all of you.

Walter Cimini, my incredible partner in this life, promised me from the beginning that he'd always keep a smile on my face—and he's never let me down. I'm so grateful to have found you, and I thank you every day for your love and support and for being my best friend.

My children, Bobby, Olivia, and Troy, have lovingly endured endless hours of me working to create a better life for us. You inspire me to do more in this world and to show others that they can as well. Each of you is a gift I am so grateful for. May you create the lives and the versions of yourselves that bring you peace, love, and happiness always.

And finally, to Mom and Dad, for instilling in me, since the day I was born, the belief that I can do whatever I set my mind to. For always believing in me, having my back, encouraging me to pursue my dreams, and of course, for giving me this life and all the opportunity in it. Thank you.

ABOUT LISA CAMPBELL

Lisa Campbell, Canada's Profit Coach, says, "Money isn't complicated. Your relationship with it is!" Combining knowledge from her profit strategy training and her own business experiences, Lisa has coached hundreds of bookkeepers and entrepreneurs on how to build a profitable, systemized, and sustainable business by changing their relationship with money to create more profit doing the business they love.

As a profit strategist, Lisa's goal is to help as many businesses as she can earn more profit. She's found that the fastest way to do this is to coach the bookkeepers, accountants, and business coaches that help these businesses to set up a system that prioritizes profit.

Lisa is passionate about showing bookkeepers and entrepreneurs how they can work together to create more profitability all around.

Lisa lives in Burlington, Ontario, Canada, with her three children.

Connect with Lisa:
LisaCampbellProfitCoach.com
Facebook: https://www.Facebook.com/LCProfitCoach
Instagram: @LCProfitCoach
Clubhouse: @LCProfitCoach

Free 9-Day Live Training!

ACCELERATOR METHOD MASTERCLASS SERIES

A few times a year Lisa puts on an incredible FREE 9-day masterclass series with lots of fantastic bonuses!

Save your seat for the next one!

www.accelerate2advisor.com

Made in the USA
Las Vegas, NV
10 August 2022

53034359R00059